BOOKWORMS CL

Pearl

STORIES FOR READING CIRCLES
Stage 2 (700 headwords)
Stage 3 (1000 headwords)

The seven short stories in this book come from different volumes in the Oxford Bookworms Library. There are four stories at Stage 2 and three stories at Stage 3. All have been specially chosen for Reading Circles.

There are many different kinds of story in this book. They come from many parts of the world – Malaysia, Uganda, Tanzania, America, Britain, New Zealand. There is the terror of child soldiers, and the horror of a mad revenge. There are children listening to stories, and adults who can't talk to each other. There are people looking for love and not finding it, and there are people in love – young people bravely crossing cultural boundaries to find each other. And then there are Herb and Amy, two old people whose love for each other is so deep and strong that it needs no words . . .

OXFORD BOOKWORMS LIBRARY
Series Editor: Jennifer Bassett
Founder Editor: Tricia Hedge

The Bookworms Club
for Reading Circles

THE METALS SET		THE GEMS SET
	STAGES 5 and 6	◀ Bookworms Club *Diamond*
Bookworms Club *Platinum* ▶	STAGES 4 and 5	◀ Bookworms Club *Ruby*
Bookworms Club *Gold* ▶	STAGES 3 and 4	◀ Bookworms Club *Coral*
Bookworms Club *Silver* ▶	STAGES 2 and 3	◀ Bookworms Club *Pearl*
Bookworms Club *Bronze* ▶	STAGES 1 and 2	

The two sets of Bookworms Club books, *Metals* and *Gems*, offer different progressions through the Bookworms language stages.

The Metals Set starts at Stage 1 and moves at a gentler pace upwards through the levels to Stage 5. Each volume has five stories at the lower level and two stories at the higher level. The stories offer a wide variety of themes to interest young adults, and *The Metals Set* is an ideal starting point for students new to Reading Circles.

The Gems Set starts at Stage 2 and moves at a faster pace upwards through the levels to Stage 6. Each volume has four stories at the lower level and three stories at the higher level. This faster progression and the more mature thematic matter of the stories, many of which are taken from the *Bookworms World Stories* collections, are suitable for more advanced students.

~

BOOKWORMS CLUB

STORIES FOR READING CIRCLES

THE GEMS SET

Editor:
Mark Furr

OXFORD UNIVERSITY PRESS

OXFORD
UNIVERSITY PRESS

Great Clarendon Street, Oxford, OX2 6DP, United Kingdom

Oxford University Press is a department of the University of Oxford.
It furthers the University's objective of excellence in research, scholarship,
and education by publishing worldwide. Oxford is a registered trade
mark of Oxford University Press in the UK and in certain other countries

Dora's Turn © Jackee Budesta Batanda 2004; *Callus* © Janet Tay Hui Ching 2003
The Silk © Joy Cowley 1965; *Breaking Loose* © M. G. Vassanji 1992

This simplified edition © Oxford University Press 2011

The moral rights of the author have been asserted

First published in Oxford Bookworms 2011

10 9 8 7 6 5 4 3 2 1

ISBN: 978 0 19 472004 5

Printed in China

For more information on the Oxford Bookworms Library,
visit www.oup.com/elt/bookworms

ACKNOWLEDGEMENTS

The publishers are grateful to the following for permission to abridge and simplify copyright texts: Jackee
Budesta Batanda for *Dora's Turn*; Janet Tay Hui Ching for *Callus*; both the former selected from
the winning entries of the Commonwealth Short Story Competition administered by the
Commonwealth Broadcasting Association and funded by the Commonwealth Foundation; Joy
Cowley for *The Silk*; M. G. Vassanji and McClelland & Stewart Ltd for *Breaking Loose*, from *Uhuru
Street* (McClelland & Stewart Ltd, 1992 / Heinemann International Literature and textbooks, 1991)

CONTENTS

SOURCE OF STORIES

The seven stories in this book were originally published in different volumes in the OXFORD BOOKWORMS LIBRARY. They appeared in the following titles:

Callus
    Janet Tay Hui Ching, from *Cries from the Heart: Stories from Around the World*. Retold by Jennifer Bassett

Dora's Turn
    Jackee Budesta Batanda, from *Cries from the Heart: Stories from Around the World*. Retold by Jennifer Bassett

The Memento
    O. Henry, from *New Yorkers*. Retold by Diane Mowat

The Cask of Amontillado
    Edgar Allan Poe, from *The Pit and the Pendulum and Other Stories*. Retold by John Escott

The Story-Teller
    Saki, from *Tooth and Claw*. Retold by Rosemary Border

Breaking Loose
    M. G. Vassanji, from *Dancing with Strangers: Stories from Africa*. Retold by Clare West

The Silk
    Joy Cowley, from *The Long White Cloud: Stories from New Zealand*. Retold by Christine Lindop

~

Welcome
to Reading Circles

Reading Circles are small groups of students who meet in the classroom to talk about stories. Each student has a special role, and usually there are six roles in the Circle:

 Discussion Leader   Word Master

 Summarizer   Passage Person

 Connector   Culture Collector

Each role has a role sheet with notes and questions which will help you prepare for your Reading Circle discussions in the classroom. You can read more about the roles and the role sheets on pages 83 to 89 at the back of this book.

The stories in this book have been specially chosen for Reading Circles. They have many different themes, and students everywhere enjoy reading them and talking about them in their Circle. Everybody's ideas are important; there are no 'right' or 'wrong' answers when you are talking about stories.

Enjoy the reading, enjoy the talking – and discover the magic of Reading Circles …

Mark Furr
Hawaii, January 2011

Callus

Some people don't find it easy to talk about their feelings. If they have never talked about them, it can be hard to begin. And year after year, it gets harder and harder – just like a callus on the skin.

A wife watches while her husband packs his suitcase. A great change is coming into their lives, but maybe it is easier to talk about the suitcase . . .

Callus

Retold by Jennifer Bassett

She watched him pack his clothes and his wedding suit into his old suitcase. She could smell his cologne. When did he last wear cologne? Ah, at their wedding. It smelt strange then too. She never wore perfume. What use was perfume to a working woman like her? And married women who wear perfume are looking for lovers, trying to catch other men. That's what people say. She already had a good, hard-working husband with a shop of his own. What more can a woman want? She began to feel better now, thinking about her good luck.

Lost in her thoughts, she jumped at the sound of the suitcase shutting. His eyes went slowly round the room, looking for – what? She looked up at him.

'I put out all the clothes that you need,' she said. 'And you can't get any more in. It's a small suitcase.'

He looked at her for a moment. A Chinese girl like any other Chinese girl – small eyes, flat nose, smooth pale skin, and long straight hair, now pinned up tidily, in the way of married Chinese ladies. She wore her usual light blue samfoo. No, she was not a beauty, he thought, but she was a hard worker. His family was right when they said to him, 'She will make a very good wife, work hard for you, give you many sons.'

And it was true. He never had to complain about her, not once, from the day they married and moved into their new home, with his future in the same suitcase. Her face was the same now as it was then, neither soft nor hard, never showing what she felt or needed. He didn't know what she needed. And he never asked.

'It's a good suitcase. It's lasted a long time,' he said.

'Yes, I suppose. But it's still small.'

She got up from the bed and shook the pillows. They needed washing, she thought. Yes, wash it away, the dust and dirt of yesterday. Their past married life together. In the future nothing would ever be the same again.

'It's enough,' he said. 'I don't have so many things to put in it.' He put the suitcase on the floor, ready to go.

She looked at him, still smelling his cologne. Maybe it was the cologne that was making her feel afraid. She had to talk to him, tell him about her feelings. But she was a hard-working Chinese woman . . . and hard-working Chinese women must not have feelings.

'Is she waiting for you there?' she asked slowly.

'You mean the hotel?'

'Yes. I suppose the ceremony starts soon?'

She picked up one of the pillows and took off its cover. Yes, it needed washing. She wanted to get hold of him and shake him, scream and shout, and fall on her knees in front of him, crying 'No, no, please stay, don't go. I'll be a better wife. I'll work harder. I'll work as hard as two wives.' But she just stood there, saying nothing, doing nothing, her face showing nothing.

'I suppose,' he said.

'You'll be back in two days?'

He didn't want to talk about her feelings. She never did before. But then it wasn't every day that your husband brought home a new wife. A younger wife. Only nineteen. And beautiful because she was young and happy, and had big dark brown eyes – bright eyes. He only saw her once before he decided, but he remembered her eyes. It would be good to add her to the family, he thought. Now he would have two hard-working wives, one stronger than the other, but the young one would be like a new flower in the house. He picked up his suitcase.

'Yes, perhaps sooner. I don't know,' he said.

'I'll take care of the shop,' she said. 'When you come back . . . with her . . . I'll have some jobs for her to do.'

She sat on the bed again, suddenly feeling tired and old. He didn't understand. No one understood. She couldn't ask him not to go. People would say that she was wrong even to ask him.

'Of course,' he said. He was pleased that she thought of business. Business was important. He had many mouths to feed. He opened the door and turned to her.

'Today is a great day for our family. Not everyone is rich enough to have two wives. And there will be more sons to continue the family name.' He smiled at her.

'Yes. Not everyone . . . Husband?' She looked up at him, waiting, hoping.

'I have to go now. I'm late.' He did not want her to say anything. He never asked questions about her feelings because he was afraid of the answers. It was easier to pretend that she was happy all the time.

'Your suitcase. It's old. You need a new one.'

Thankfully, he turned away. No questions asked, no answers needed.

'Perhaps I will get a new one after all,' he said. He left the room and the door closed quietly behind him.

WORD FOCUS

Match each word with an appropriate meaning.

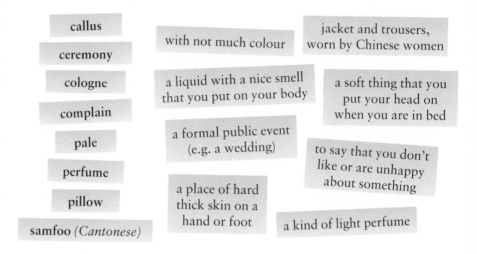

callus

ceremony

cologne

complain

pale

perfume

pillow

samfoo *(Cantonese)*

with not much colour

jacket and trousers, worn by Chinese women

a liquid with a nice smell that you put on your body

a soft thing that you put your head on when you are in bed

a formal public event (e.g. a wedding)

to say that you don't like or are unhappy about something

a place of hard thick skin on a hand or foot

a kind of light perfume

After the man left, perhaps his wife went on thinking about the past and the future. Use six of the eight words from the list above to complete her thoughts. (Use one word in each gap.)

'I remember the day we were married. The _____ was at a hotel. On that day, I wore a beautiful dress, not this old _____ that I now wear every day. I remember the smell. My new husband wore _____ on our wedding day, but I didn't wear _____. My family taught me that a wife does not need to worry about smelling good or wearing jewelry. These things are useless to a hard-working wife. Oh, what will she be like, this new young wife? Will she be beautiful, with smooth _____ skin, and bright eyes? Oh, I must stop thinking about it . . . I must go and wash these _____, wash away the dust and dirt of yesterday . . .'

STORY FOCUS 1

Marriage is an important idea in almost every culture. What is special about a wedding day in your culture? Make a list, using these ideas to help you.

special ceremonies / wedding clothes / special foods

1 _____   4 _____

2 _____   5 _____

3 _____   6 _____

STORY FOCUS 2

In different cultures, there are different ways to choose a husband or wife. Think about these questions, and write a few sentences to explain your answers. Then share your answers with another student.

1 How do you think that marriage partners were chosen in this story?
2 Is this similar to or different from the way marriage partners are chosen in your own culture?

Dora's Turn

~

War is, in any place, at any time, a terrible thing. The heart cries out against the killing, but it still happens.

Somewhere in Uganda, Acayo and her friend Dora are fighting in a war. They carry big AK-47 guns, and they know all about death and killing, pain and fear. They are children, twelve years old . . .

Dora's Turn

Retold by Jennifer Bassett

The little boy's cries are getting quieter, weaker. I can only just hear the words. 'Please, please . . . ah, no, no, no . . . Help me . . . help . . .'

Now there is a louder voice, the voice of Mad Tiger, our commander. He is fourteen years old.

'Hit him harder!' he shouts at us. 'Get closer to him. Use your whips – harder!'

The noise of our whips through the air is louder than the boy's cries.

'Our war is good,' shouts Mad Tiger. 'We must clean out bad people. We are soldiers – no escaping, no running away, everyone must fight.'

The other commanders smoke their cigarettes under a tree.

'Go on,' they laugh at us, 'get blood on your hands.'

The boy on the ground stops moving. Our whips are still. It is over.

I feel ill. There is something hard in my throat, like a stone. I can't breathe. My friend Dora also tried to escape, and she'll be next. They will order me to kill her. Dora and I have been close. We are both twelve years old. Dora, who is going to be a doctor after the war . . . Dora, who wants to save lives, to stop the killing . . . Dora, who has been my friend when I wake in the night, screaming, because I can see the faces of all the people that I have killed . . .

The AK-47 is heavy on my shoulder, and I stand, waiting . . . waiting for Dora's turn, and the stone in my throat gets bigger.

'Acayo!' Mad Tiger shouts. I turn and look at him, hiding the fear in my eyes. It is a crime to show fear. My mouth is shut in a hard line. This helps to stop the tears coming into my eyes.

'Yes, *Afande*,' I say quietly. My voice must not be angry or unhappy or afraid, just quiet. That way he will not hear my fear. I give a soldier's salute to my commander, take my gun off my shoulder, and hold it up against my body. The gun points up to the black sky and the full moon. And the moon looks down at us, watching these deaths.

Mad Tiger smiles, his teeth shining white in the moonlight. He looks pleased. 'Are you ready?'

I cannot speak, but I nod my head.

They push Dora forward, and she falls on the ground in front of me, trembling. She is so small and thin, like a flower shaking in the wind. Our eyes meet. We cannot use words so we speak with our eyes. I don't want to do this, my eyes tell her.

But Mad Tiger and the other commanders are watching us, so I take Dora's arm and pull her to her feet. I want to ask her questions – Why did she try to escape without me? Why, Dora, why? We have always known each other's secrets before tonight.

Holding Dora's arm, I push her towards the trees. The killing will happen there, behind the trees, where no one can see. They are watching me, I can feel their eyes on my back. Perhaps they are following us, but I can't turn round to look.

My legs are trembling. The stone in my throat gets bigger. My hands are hot and wet, and my fingers are making red marks on Dora's arm.

I take my hand away. I can't do this, not to Dora. We've been here together for three years.

'Don't be sorry,' Dora whispers. 'You have to do it. Everybody has to do it.'

She mustn't talk, someone will hear. Afraid, I look behind me. We are alone. Quickly, I push Dora further into the trees. We stop.

I'm cold. I'm afraid.

'I can't do this,' I cry.

'You must,' Dora whispers. 'Or they'll kill you too.'

'Then they must kill us both.' The stone in my throat goes away with those words. 'You're my friend. We can run away . . . look for the government's soldiers . . . ask for help . . .' I speak excitedly. We can do it.

'Acayo,' Dora says, 'stop this talk. You know we—'

At that moment comes the sound of heavy guns behind us, where Mad Tiger and the others are.

'What . . .?' whispers Dora.

Suddenly I understand. Those are government army

guns, not our guns. A helicopter gunship has found Mad Tiger's group.

'This is our chance!' I drop my gun and take hold of Dora's hand. 'Run!'

Dora stares at me, not sure.

'Do you still want to be a doctor?' I shout.

Suddenly Dora's feet come to life again. And the ground under our running feet trembles.

WORD FOCUS

Match each word with an appropriate meaning.

breathe	to shake because you are cold, afraid, or ill	a long piece of rope for hitting animals
government		
salute (*n*)	fighting between countries, or between groups of people	the people who make laws and control the country
throat		
tremble	to take in and let out air through the nose and mouth	
war	the inside part of your neck, where food and air go down	the sign that soldiers make, lifting the hand to the head
whip (*n*)		

Many years later, perhaps Dora tells a friend the story of her escape from death. Use five of the seven words from the list above to fill the gaps. (Use one word in each gap.)

'I could hear the little boy's cries. He was getting weaker as the others hit him with their _____s. I heard the commanders laughing, and then our commander, Mad Tiger, shouted at Acayo. She gave him a soldier's _____, and the others pushed me forward. I began to _____ with fear and fell on the ground. Acayo didn't want to kill me, but she had to. We both knew that. But she couldn't do it. When we were behind the trees, she began to talk about running away. Then we suddenly heard the sound of heavy guns. They were _____ army guns – a helicopter gunship had found Mad Tiger's group. So we escaped. But it was a terrible time. Too many children had to fight and die in that _____.'

STORY FOCUS 1

In a story, the narrator is a character who tells the story. What do you think about the narrator in *Dora's Turn*? Choose one adjective for each first gap, and then finish the sentences in your own words.

afraid, angry, brave, clever, excited, frightened, kind, nervous, sad, strong, unhappy

1 I think that the narrator was _____ because _____.
2 The narrator was _____ when _____.
3 When the narrator says she met Dora's eyes, I think she felt _____ because _____.
4 When she is ordered to kill Dora, I believe that the narrator was _____ because _____.

STORY FOCUS 2

Match these halves of sentences to make a paragraph of five sentences. Who is the narrator here?

1 When I was fourteen years old, . . .
2 Some of my soldiers were only twelve years old, but . . .
3 When some of my young soldiers tried to escape, . . .
4 Sometimes we even had to kill members of our group because . . .
5 It was necessary to do these things if . . .

6 . . . I ordered their friends to beat them with whips.
7 . . . we wanted to beat the government's army.
8 . . . I became commander of a group of young soldiers.
9 . . . in a war, soldiers must always obey their commander's orders.
10 . . . they had to learn to kill if they wanted to stay alive.

The Memento

~

Everybody keeps a memento or two – some small thing that reminds them of a person, a place, an event in the past. Perhaps it is a baby's first pair of shoes, or a ticket from a show, or a love gift.

Rosalie Ray, a young actress in New York, has a story to tell her friend, Miss D'Armande. It's the story of a memento that brings back a past she would like to forget . . .

The Memento

Retold by Diane Mowat

The window of Miss D'Armande's room looked out onto Broadway and its theatres. But Lynnette D'Armande turned her chair round and sat with her back to Broadway. She was an actress, and needed the Broadway theatres, but Broadway did not need her.

She was staying in the Hotel Thalia. Actors go there to rest for the summer and then try to get work for the autumn when the little theatres open again. Miss D'Armande's room in this hotel was a small one, but in it there were many mementoes of her days in the theatre, and there were also pictures of some of her best friends. She looked at one of these pictures now, and smiled at it.

'I'd like to know where Lee is now,' she said to herself.

She was looking at a picture of Miss Rosalie Ray, a very beautiful young woman. In the picture, Miss Ray was wearing a very short skirt and she was sitting on a swing. Every night in the theatre she went high in the air on her swing, over the heads of all the people. When she did this, all the men in the theatre got very excited and stood up. This was because, when her long beautiful legs were high in the air, her yellow garter flew off and fell down to the men below. She did this every evening, and every evening a hundred hands went up to catch the garter. She did other things. She sang, she danced, but when she got onto her swing, all the men stood up. Miss Ray did not have to try very hard to find work in the theatre.

After two years of this, Miss D'Armande remembered, Miss Ray suddenly left the theatre and went to live in the country.

And seventeen minutes after Miss D'Armande said, 'I'd like to know where Lee is now', somebody knocked on the door.

It was, of course, Rosalie Ray.

'Come in,' Miss D'Armande called, and Miss Ray came in. Yes, it was Rosalie. She took off her hat, and Miss D'Armande could see that she looked very tired and unhappy.

'I've got the room above you,' Rosalie said. 'They told me at the desk downstairs that you were here.'

'I've been here since the end of April,' Lynnette replied. 'I begin work again next week, out in a small town. But you left the theatre three months ago, Lee. Why are you here?'

'I'll tell you, Lynn, but give me a drink first.' Miss D'Armande passed a bottle to her friend.

'Ah, that's good!' said Rosalie. 'My first drink for three months. Yes, Lynn, I left the theatre because I was tired of the life, and because I was tired of men – well, the men who come to the theatre. You know we have to fight them off all the time. They're animals! They ask you to go out with them, they buy you a drink or two – and then they think that they can do what they want! It's terrible! And we work hard, we get very little money for it, we wait to get to the top – and it never happens. But most of all, I left because of the men.

'Well, I saved two hundred dollars and when summer came, I left the theatre and went to a little village by the sea on Long Island. I planned to stay there for the summer, and then learn how to be a better actress.

'But there was another person who was staying in the same house – the Reverend Arthur Lyle. Yes, Lynn, a man of the church! When I saw him for the first time, I fell in love with him at once. He was a fine man and he had a wonderful voice!

'Well, it's only a short story, Lynn. A month later we decided to marry. We planned to live in a little house near the church, with lots of flowers and animals.

'No, I didn't tell him that I was an actress. I wanted to forget it and to put that life behind me.

'Oh, I was happy! I went to church, I helped the women in the village. Arthur and I went for long walks – and that little village was the best place in the world. I wanted to live there for ever . . .

'But one morning, the old woman who worked in the house began to talk about Arthur. She thought that he was wonderful, too. But then she told me that Arthur was in love once before, and that it ended unhappily. She said that, in his desk, he kept a memento – something which belonged to the girl. Sometimes he took it out and looked at it. But she didn't know what it was – and his desk was locked.

'That afternoon I asked him about it.

' "Ida," he said, (of course, I used my real name there) "it was before I knew you, and I never met her. It was different from my love for you."

' "Was she beautiful?" I asked.

' "She was very beautiful," replied Arthur.

' "Did you see her often?"

' "About ten times," he said.

' "And this memento – did she send it to you?"

' "It came to me from her," he said.

' "Why did you never meet her?" I asked.

' "She was far above me," he answered. "But, Ida, it's finished. You're not angry, are you?"

' "Why, no. I love you ten times more than before." And I did, Lynn. Can you understand that? What a beautiful love that was! He never met her, never spoke to her, but he loved her, and wanted nothing from her. He was different from other men, I thought – a really good man!

'About four o'clock that afternoon, Arthur had to go out. The door of his room was open, his desk was unlocked, and I decided to look at this memento. I opened the desk and slowly I took out the box and opened it.

'I took one look at that memento, and then I went to my room and packed my suitcase. My wonderful Arthur, this really good man, was no different from all the other men!'

'But, Lee, what was in the box?' Miss D'Armande asked.

'It was one of my yellow garters!' cried Miss Ray.

23

Word Focus

Use the clues below and complete this crossword with words from the story.

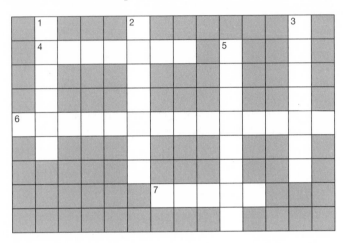

Across

4 Rosalie was an _____, a woman who performs in plays and shows.

6 When Rosalie saw the Reverend for the first time, she _____ _____ _____ _____ him at once, and wanted to marry him. *(four words)*

7 Every night in the theatre, Rosalie wore a short skirt and went high in the air on a _____.

Down

1 The men stood up every night to catch Rosalie's _____ when it flew off her long, beautiful legs.

2 A _____ is something which helps you remember somebody. Arthur kept one in a box in his desk.

3 Rosalie was tired of the men who came to the _____ every night.

5 Arthur used the title 'the _____' before his name, because he was a man of the church.

STORY FOCUS 1

What do you think of the people in this story? Choose some names from the list and complete these sentences in your own words.

Lynnette D'Armande / Rosalie Ray / the Reverend Arthur Lyle

1 I think _____ was happy when _____.
2 I thought _____ was right to _____.
3 I thought _____ was wrong to _____.
4 I thought _____ made a mistake when _____.
5 I felt sorry for _____ because _____.

STORY FOCUS 2

After Rosalie's visit to her room, perhaps Lynnette wrote her diary for that day. Here are some sentences from it. Choose one adjective from the list for the first gap, and then write as much as you like to finish the sentences.

afraid, angry, excited, happy, jealous, lonely, lucky, sad, sorry, surprised, unlucky

• Before Lee came to visit, I was thinking about her, and I felt _____ because _____.

• When she came into the room, I was _____ because _____.

• When I heard Lee's story about meeting the Reverend, I felt _____ because _____.

• After Lee told me about the Reverend's memento, I felt _____ for her because _____.

• Finally, when I heard that Lee had left the Reverend, I felt _____ because _____.

The
Cask of
Amontillado

~

Some men never forget an insult, real or imagined.
They will wait and watch for the perfect moment
to punish the person who has insulted them.

It is carnival night, and Montresor believes the
perfect moment has come to punish Fortunato.
He will be clever, and secret, and Fortunato will
suspect nothing. He will use a story about sherry
wine to bring him to the house – yes, yes, a cask
of Amontillado will be the perfect thing . . .

EDGAR ALLAN POE

The Cask of Amontillado

Retold by John Escott

Fortunato did and said a thousand things to hurt me. But when he insulted me, I knew that it was time to punish him. 'But I must do it cleverly and secretly,' I thought. 'Only Fortunato himself must know that I am punishing him.'

I was as friendly to Fortunato as before, of course. I went on smiling at him, and he did not know that I was smiling at the thought of his death.

Both he and I liked and bought fine wine. Fortunato knew very little about other things, but he did know about wine and sherry wine. And so did I.

One evening, during the city's carnival, I met my friend in the street. He was dressed in carnival clothes and smelled strongly of wine.

'My dear Fortunato!' I said. 'What luck to meet you! I have bought a cask of Amontillado – but now, well, I'm not so sure that it *is* Amontillado.'

'Amontillado?' said Fortunato. 'No, no! Nobody sells the best sherry in the middle of carnival. No, no, no!'

'I was stupid,' I said. 'I paid the full Amontillado price, and did not ask you to try it first. But I couldn't find you, and I was afraid of losing it to another buyer. So, the cask is already in my vaults.'

'Amontillado!' he said.

'Perhaps,' I said. 'But I must be sure. I can see that you are on your way to a carnival party. I'll go and see Luchresi. He will tell me—'

'Luchresi does not know the difference between Amontillado and any other sherry wine,' he said.

'Really? But some people say that he knows wine as well as you do.'

'Come, let's go,' he said.

'Where to?'

'To your vaults,' he said.

'My friend, no,' I said. 'I can hear that you have a bad cough, and my vaults are terribly cold and wet.'

'My cough is nothing,' Fortunato said. 'Let's go. Amontillado! Never! Your wine-seller is stealing your money. And as for Luchresi – what does he know about Amontillado?'

He took my arm, and we walked quickly to my house.

There was no one at home because my servants were out enjoying themselves at the carnival. I took Fortunato through the building and down the stairs into the vaults. Here were the tombs of the Montresors – my family.

'The Amontillado?' Fortunato said. He began to cough in the cold, damp air.

'It's further on,' I said. 'How long have you had that cough?'

He went on coughing for some time before he could answer me. 'It is nothing,' he said, at last.

My friend was full of wine, and found walking difficult.

The little bells on his carnival suit made ringing noises when he moved. He began to cough again.

'We'll go back,' I said. 'You must not get ill. You have family, friends, you are loved, needed – you must take care of yourself. We'll go back. I can go to Luchresi—'

'Stop!' he said. 'The cough is nothing. It will not kill me. I shall not die from a cough.'

'That's true,' I said. 'But you must be careful. Take a drink from this bottle of Medoc. It is a good wine and will warm you. Here you are, drink this!'

I opened the bottle and gave it to him. 'I drink,' he said, 'to all the dead Montresors sleeping around us.' And he drank.

'And I drink to your long life,' I said.

Again he took my arm and we walked on.

'These vaults are very large,' he said.

'The Montresor family is a very old one. There have been a great many of us.' I was warmed by the Medoc, and the wine was making Fortunato's eyes bright. We walked on, past casks and bottles of wine, deep into the vaults. I stopped again and held his arm.

'We are under the river now,' I said. 'See how wet the walls are here. Come, we will go back before it is too late. Your cough—'

'It is nothing,' he said. 'Let's go on. But first, another drink to keep us warm.'

I took another bottle of wine and gave it to him. He drank it all without stopping. His eyes were even brighter, and he laughed.

'Now, let's go on to the Amontillado,' he said.

We went on, and down, and came into the deepest vault. Around three walls, from floor to ceiling, were the bones of the dead. Many more bones lay on the floor. Cut into the fourth wall was a smaller vault.

Fortunato held up his torch and looked into the blackness, but could see nothing.

'Go in,' I told him. 'You will find the Amontillado in there.'

He went inside and I followed him. In three steps he was at the back wall of the vault, and he stood there, looking stupid. On the wall were two metal rings and a chain with a lock. Before he could do anything, I put the chain around him and locked it to the rings.

'Put your hand on the wall, Fortunato,' I said. 'How wet it is! How *very* wet! Once more I ask, why don't you go back? No? Then I must leave you. But first I must try to make you comfortable.'

'The – the Amontillado!' my friend said. He did not understand.

'True,' I said. 'The Amontillado.'

Hidden under some of the bones on the floor were stones and other things for building a wall. I took them across to the small vault and began to work quickly.

Before the wall was half a metre high, Fortunato began to make soft crying noises. Then he was silent for some time. I worked on busily, building the wall higher and higher. Then I heard him again. He was pulling the chain and shaking it, but I knew the lock was strong.

The wall was now as high as my neck. I held my torch higher, to see his face. He began to scream, long high screams, filled with terror. I listened, worrying. No, we were too deep under the ground. No sounds would escape from this vault. I screamed back at Fortunato, longer and louder. Then he stopped.

By midnight the wall was nearly finished. There was one last heavy stone. I had it almost in place when I heard a soft but terrible laugh.

Then Fortunato's sad voice said, 'Ha! Ha! Ha! A very good joke. We will laugh about it often when we are drinking our wine.'

'The Amontillado!' I said.

'Ha! Ha! Yes, the Amontillado. But it is getting late. My wife and friends are waiting for me. Let's go now, Montresor.'

'Yes,' I said, 'Let's go.'

'For the love of God, Montresor!'

'Yes,' I said, 'For the love of God.'

I waited for an answer. None came.

'Fortunato!' I called.

No answer. I called again.

'Fortunato!'

Still no answer. I pushed my torch through the gap in the wall and let it fall. Still nothing. I put the last stone in place, and then in front of the new wall I put the bones of the dead.

For fifty years, nobody has moved them.

WORD FOCUS

Match each word with an appropriate meaning. Then use six of the thirteen words to complete the sentences below (use one word in each gap).

bell	a large wooden container for drink	very great fear
bone		to hurt someone because they did something wrong
carnival	an alcoholic drink made from grapes	
cask		someone who works in another person's house
ceiling	a metal thing that makes a noise when someone hits it	
chain		a small stone building for a dead person
cough	to say something bad about somebody	to send out air from the mouth in a noisy way
insult (v)		
punish	one of the hard white parts inside your body	a lot of metal rings joined together in a line
servant		
terror	a party for everybody in the streets, with singing, music and dancing	the part of the room that is over your head
tomb		
wine		

1 Montresor was angry because Fortunato had _____ed him.
2 Montresor decided to _____ Fortunato for his insult.
3 Montresor met Fortunato at the city's _____ where Fortunato had been drinking wine.
4 Fortunato was ill. He had a bad _____.
5 The _____s of Montresor's dead family members were in the vault along with the wine.
6 Fortunato felt _____ while Montresor was building the wall.

STORY FOCUS

Here are three short passages from the story. Read them and answer the questions.

'We'll go back,' I said. 'You must not get ill. You have family, friends, you are loved, needed – you must take care of yourself. We'll go back. I can go to Luchresi—'

1 Who says these words in the story, and to whom?
2 Where does this conversation take place?
3 Why do you think the speaker mentions 'Luchresi'?

'And I drink to your long life.'

4 Who is speaking, and to whom?
5 Why do you think the speaker says these words?
6 Do you think the listener believes the speaker? Why or why not?

'Ha! Ha! Ha! A very good joke. We will laugh about it often when we are drinking our wine.'

7 Who says these words in the story, and to whom?
8 What is happening when the speaker says these words?
9 Why do you think that the speaker calls this a 'joke'?

The
Story-Teller

~

Children love stories – funny, scary, happy, or sad. They will sit quietly and listen for hours – to a good story, told by a good story-teller.

Three small children are travelling in a train with their aunt. There is not much to do, and not much to look at. The children are bored and restless, and need something to amuse them. Their aunt decides to tell them a story . . .

The Story-Teller

Retold by Rosemary Border

It was a hot, airless afternoon. The train was slow and the next stop was nearly an hour away. The people in the train were hot and tired. There were three small children and their aunt, and a tall man, who was a bachelor. The bachelor did not know the little family, and he did not want to know them.

The aunt and the children talked, but it was not a real conversation. It was more like a battle with a small housefly which will not go away. When the aunt spoke to the children, she always began with 'Don't . . .' When the children spoke to her, they always began with 'Why . . .' The bachelor said nothing aloud.

The small boy opened his mouth and closed it again. It made an interesting little noise, so he did it again. Open. Close. Open. Close. 'Don't do that, Cyril,' said the aunt. 'Come and look out of the window.'

The boy closed his mouth and sat next to the window. He looked out at the green fields and trees.

'Why is that man taking those sheep out of that field?' he asked suddenly.

'Perhaps he's taking them to another field where there is more grass,' said the aunt. It was not a very good answer, and the boy knew it.

'But there is lots of grass in that field,' he said. 'The field is full of grass, Aunt. Why doesn't the man leave his sheep in that field?'

'I suppose the grass in the other field is better,' answered the aunt.

'Why is it better?' asked Cyril at once.

'Oh, look at those cows!' cried the aunt. There were cows in nearly all the fields along the railway line. Cyril did not look at the cows. He wanted an answer to his question.

'Why is the grass in the other field better?' he said again.

The bachelor gave them an angry look. The aunt saw him. He's a hard, unkind man, she thought. He doesn't like children. She searched for a suitable answer to Cyril's question, but could not find one.

The smaller girl began to say some words from a song:

'On the road to Mandalay, where the happy children play,' she began.

Then she stopped. She could not remember any more words, so she said the first words again, quietly but very clearly. Then she said them again. And again. And again.

The bachelor looked angrily at the girl, and then at the aunt.

'Come here and sit down quietly,' the aunt said quickly to the children. 'I'm going to tell you a story.'

The children moved slowly towards the aunt's seat. They already looked bored. Clearly, the aunt was not a famous story-teller.

The story was horribly uninteresting. It was about a little girl. She was not a beautiful child, but she was always very, very good. Everybody loved her because she was good. Finally, she fell into a lake and her friends saved her because she was so good, and they loved her so much.

'Did they only save her because she was good?' asked the bigger girl. 'Shouldn't we save bad people too, if they fall into a lake?' The bachelor wanted to ask the same question, but he said nothing.

'Well, yes, we should,' said the aunt. 'But I'm sure the little girl's friends ran specially fast because they loved her so much.'

'That was the stupidest story that I've ever heard,' said the bigger girl.

'I didn't listen after the first few words,' said Cyril, 'because it was so stupid.'

The smaller girl was already quietly repeating the words of her song for the twentieth time.

'You're not very successful as a story-teller,' the bachelor said suddenly from his corner.

The aunt looked at him in angry surprise. 'It's not easy to tell stories that children can understand,' she answered coldly.

'I don't agree with you,' said the bachelor.

'Perhaps *you* would like to tell them a story,' said the aunt. She gave him a cold little smile.

'Yes – tell us a story,' said the bigger girl.

'A long time ago,' began the bachelor, 'there was a little girl called Bertha, who was extraordinarily good.

She always worked well at school. She always obeyed her teachers and her parents. She was never late, never dirty, and always ate all her vegetables. She was polite, she was tidy, and she never, never told lies.'

'Oh,' said the children. They were beginning to look bored already.

'Was she pretty?' asked the smaller girl.

'No,' said the bachelor. 'She wasn't pretty. But she was horribly good.'

'Horribly good. I like that!' said Cyril. The children began to look more interested. The words 'horrible' and 'good' together was a new idea for them, and it pleased them.

'Bertha was always good,' continued the bachelor. 'Because she was so good, Bertha had three medals. There was the "Never Late" medal. There was the "Politeness" medal. And there was the medal for the "Best Child in the World". They were very large medals. Bertha always wore them on her dress, and they clinked as she walked along. She was the only child in her town who had three medals. So everybody knew that she must be an extra good child.'

'Horribly good,' repeated Cyril happily.

'Everybody talked about Bertha's goodness. The king of that country heard about her, and he was very pleased. "Because Bertha is so good," he said, "she may come and walk in my palace gardens every Friday afternoon." The king's gardens were famous. They were large and very beautiful, and children were usually forbidden to go in them.'

'Were there any sheep in the palace gardens?' asked Cyril.

'No,' said the bachelor, 'there were no sheep.'

'Why weren't there any sheep?' asked Cyril at once.

The aunt gave a little smile, and waited with interest for the bachelor's answer.

'There were no sheep in the king's gardens,' explained the bachelor, 'because the king's mother had once had a dream. In her dream a voice said to her, "Your son will be killed by a sheep, or by a clock falling on him." That is why the king never kept a sheep in his gardens or a clock in his palace.'

The aunt thought secretly that this was a very clever answer, but she stayed silent.

'Was the king killed by a sheep, or by a clock?' asked the bigger girl.

'He is still alive,' said the bachelor calmly, 'so we don't know if the dream was true or not. But, although there were no sheep, there were lots of little pigs running around everywhere.'

'What colour were the pigs?' asked the smaller girl.

'Black with white faces, white with black faces, all black, grey and white, and some were all white.'

The bachelor stopped for a moment, while the children's imaginations took in these wonderful pictures. Then he went on again,

'Bertha was sorry that there were no flowers in the palace gardens. She had promised her aunts that she would not pick any of the kind king's flowers. She wanted very much to be good and to keep her promise. So she was very cross when she found that there were no flowers to pick.'

'Why weren't there any flowers?'

'Because the pigs had eaten them all,' said the bachelor immediately. 'The gardeners had told the king that he couldn't have pigs *and* flowers, because pigs eat flowers. So the king decided to have pigs, and no flowers.'

The children thought that this was an excellent idea.

'Most people choose flowers,' said Cyril. He looked very pleased. 'But of course, pigs are *much* better than flowers.'

'There were lots of other wonderful things in the palace gardens,' the bachelor continued. 'There were lakes with gold and blue and green fish in them. There were trees with beautiful birds that could talk and say clever things. There were also birds that could sing popular songs.

'Well, on the first Friday afternoon in May, Bertha came to the king's gardens. The king's soldiers saw her beautiful white dress and her three medals for goodness, and they opened the doors to the gardens at once.

'Bertha walked up and down and enjoyed herself very much. As she walked along, the three medals on her beautiful white dress clinked against each other. She heard them clinking, and she thought: "I'm here in these lovely gardens because I am the Best Child in the World." She felt pleased and happy and very, very good.

'Just then a very big, hungry wolf came into the gardens. It wanted to catch a fat little pig for its supper.'

'What colour was the wolf?' asked the children, who were listening to the story with great interest.

'He was grey,' said the bachelor, 'with a black tongue and angry yellow eyes. He had long black claws and big, strong, yellowish teeth. The wolf was hungry. He smelled the ground with his long grey nose. Then he saw Bertha's beautiful, clean white dress and began to move quietly towards her.

'Bertha saw the wolf and she wished she had not come to the gardens. "Oh, why did I come here?" she thought. "All the bad children are safe at home. I wish I wasn't an extraordinarily good child! Then I could be safe at home too." She ran as hard as she could, and the wolf came after her on his long grey legs.

'At last Bertha managed to reach some big, sweet-smelling myrtle bushes, and she hid herself in the thickest bush. The wolf walked round and round the bushes, with his angry yellow eyes and his long black tongue. But he couldn't see Bertha because the bushes were too thick, and he couldn't smell her because the smell of the myrtle was too strong. So after a while the wolf became bored, and decided to go and catch a little pig for his supper.

'Bertha was terribly frightened. Her heart beat very fast and her body shook with fear. Her arms shook and her legs shook. Her three medals for goodness shook too. And as they shook, they clinked together. The wolf was just moving away, when he heard the medals clinking, and he stopped to listen. The medals clinked again. The wolf's yellow eyes shone, and he ran into the myrtle bushes, pulled Bertha out, and ate her. He ate everything except her shoes, a few small pieces of her dress, and the three medals for goodness.'

'Were any of the little pigs killed?' asked Cyril.

'No, they all escaped.'

'The story began badly,' said the smaller girl, 'but it finished beautifully.'

'It is the most beautiful story that I have ever heard,' said the bigger girl.

'It is the *only* beautiful story I have ever heard,' said Cyril.

The aunt did not agree. 'It was a most improper story!' she said angrily. 'You mustn't tell children stories like that! You have destroyed years of careful teaching.'

'Well,' said the bachelor. He put on his coat and picked up his bags. 'The children sat still and were quiet for ten minutes while they listened to the story. And they didn't do that for *you*.'

'I feel sorry for that woman,' thought the bachelor as he stepped down from the train at the next station. 'What will people think when those children ask her for an improper story!'

WORD FOCUS

Choose words from the list to complete these sentences (one word for each gap). There are thirteen words in the list, but only nine of them will be needed.

aunt, bachelor, bush, claws, clink, forbidden, horrible, imagination, improper, king, medal, pig, wolf

1 The man who told the story to the children in the train was a _____, a man who is not married.

2 A _____ is a piece of metal, like a coin, given to people to show that they have done something special. Bertha had three of them.

3 Because Bertha was so good, the _____ permitted her to walk in his palace gardens every Friday afternoon.

4 Bertha felt happy because the palace gardens were very beautiful, and children were usually _____ to go into the gardens.

5 When Bertha walked in the gardens, the medals on her dress _____ed together – a noise like coins knocking together.

6 After the bachelor told the children about the pigs in the gardens, he stopped for a moment while the children used their _____s to make pictures of the pigs in their heads.

7 The _____, which is a wild animal like a big dog, came into the garden to catch a fat little pig for its supper.

8 Bertha tried to hide in a myrtle _____, a plant with sweet-smelling white flowers, but the wolf heard her when her medals clinked together.

9 The children loved the man's story, but their aunt thought it was an _____ story for children.

STORY FOCUS

Later, perhaps the aunt wrote in her diary. To read her diary, match these halves of sentences to make a paragraph of ten sentences.

1 Our train journey today was long and difficult because . . .
2 The children were very noisy – they wouldn't sit quietly, and . . .
3 Finally, I tried to tell them a story, but . . .
4 After I told the story, . . .
5 I was very surprised and angry when he said this, and . . .
6 But the bachelor didn't agree with me, so . . .
7 Of course, I thought he couldn't tell a story for children because . . .
8 However, I was very surprised because . . .
9 During the story, he answered the children's questions, and . . .
10 I must say that the bachelor was a very clever story-teller, but . . .

11 . . . he is not married and wouldn't know anything about children.
12 . . . the children weren't interested in it.
13 . . . I told him that it is not easy to tell stories to children.
14 . . . he stopped at just the right moment so that the children could see the story in their imaginations.
15 . . . I asked him if he would like to tell a story.
16 . . . the ending of the story was really improper for children. Of course, how would he know? He's only a bachelor!
17 . . . the bachelor's story was unusual right from the start – the girl in his story was 'horribly good', and the children loved that idea.
18 . . . they asked me so many questions!
19 . . . the train was slow, and it was a hot airless day.
20 . . . a bachelor sitting next to us said, 'You're not very successful as a story-teller.'

Breaking
Loose

~

Where do we come from? Where do we belong?
Where is home? Easy questions, but the answers
are not always so simple. Family, culture,
history – all these things connect in different and
mysterious ways.

An Asian girl and an African man meet at a
university dance in an African country. It is the
girl's hometown, and the man is a visitor from
another country. Who is the foreigner here . . .
and does it matter?

M.G. VASSANJI

Breaking Loose

Retold by Clare West

A band called Iblis was playing on the stage. The singer and guitarist was a young Asian with long hair, now singing another popular foreign song. Close to the stage danced a group of fashionable, brightly dressed girls. Their wild way of dancing seemed to say that they were the girlfriends of the four young men in the band.

Yasmin was at the far end of the dance floor with her girlfriends. She and two of the girls were standing, because there weren't enough chairs. Sometimes she looked round at the dancers and the band, hoping to see an empty chair that she could bring over. The band was loud, the room was hot and airless, and everyone was sweating.

A well-dressed black man in a grey suit appeared out of the crowd of dancers. He came up to her and asked her to dance. She went.

Of all the girls here, why me? I don't want *to dance. I can't dance*, she thought. From the centre of the dance floor she looked back sadly at her friends, who were talking and laughing in the distance.

'I'm sorry,' he smiled. 'I took you away from your friends.'

'It's okay . . . only for a few minutes—' she began, and

blushed, realizing that was not a polite answer. *After all, I should be pleased*, she thought. *He's a professor.*

It was a dance that did not need any closeness or touching – and she was grateful for that.

'Daniel Akoto. That's my name.'

'I know . . . I'm Yasmin Rajan.'

It's all so unnecessary, she thought. *I'm not the type. Why didn't he dance with one of those girls near the stage?*

She looked at him. He danced much better than she did. She was shorter than him. Her long hair was brushed straight back from her face, and she wore a simple dress. This was the middle of her second year at the university.

'Good music,' he said.

'Yes, isn't it? I know the singer—'

'But too Western, don't you think?'

'I don't know . . .'

She felt uncomfortable with the conversation. There was the little worry too – why had he chosen her, and would he want to see her again? He was looking at her and still talking.

'. . . you're too westernized, you Asians. You like Western ways, European ways, even more than we Africans do.'

She didn't know what to reply, and felt very embarrassed.

He went on, shaking his head, 'Just listen to that song! Rolling Stones. What do you call Indian in that? Or am I missing something?'

Oh, why doesn't he stop? she thought. 'What do you mean, we're westernized?' she said angrily. 'Of course we have our own culture. We have centuries-old customs . . .'

She had stopped dancing and there were tears in her eyes. She felt under attack in the middle of the two hundred people dancing around her. She could feel their eyes burning into her, seeing her embarrassment.

She left Akoto in the middle of the dance floor and, with her back straight and her head high, returned to her friends.

The next day she waited for her punishment. A call to the university's head office, a black mark for her rudeness to a professor who was a visitor from another African country.

During lunch in the university restaurant with her friends, she saw him standing at the door, looking around the room. She took a deep breath and waited. His eyes found her and he hurried forward between the tables, laughing and calling out greetings to people as he passed. When he arrived at her table, he found an empty chair, sat down and looked at her.

'About last night . . .' he began. The other girls picked up their plates and left.

She laughed. 'You pushed them out,' she said. 'They'll hate you for that.' She wondered where she had found the confidence to speak like that to him. He was in a red shirt – expensive, she thought. He looked handsome – and harmless.

'But not for long, I hope,' he began. His smile grew wider as he looked at her. 'I've come to apologize. I asked you for a dance and then I bored you with all those ideas of mine.'

'It's okay. It's my fault too. You see . . .'

'I know, I know. An innocent Indian girl having to dance with a man! But tell me – don't you expect men to ask you to dance when you're in a dance hall with music playing?'

She smiled, a little embarrassed. 'Having girlfriends with you usually means that strangers don't come and ask . . .'

'Oh dear! I'm a foreigner, so I didn't know that! You came to have a good time with your friends but you couldn't, because of me. I'm really sorry. Look, let me show you how sorry I am. I'll take you for a drink. How about that?'

'But I don't drink . . . alcohol, I mean.'

'Don't worry. We'll find something for you.'

It was wrong of him to ask her, of course, but she found she had accepted his invitation without any worries.

When they met, as arranged, later that afternoon, he said, 'I'll take you to The Matumbi.' The Matumbi was a tea shop under a tree, half a mile from the university. It had a roof but no walls. She went in slowly, feeling a little shy. But Akoto was well known there, and the owner pulled up two chairs at a table for them.

'Are you hungry?' Akoto asked.

'No. I'll just have tea . . . perhaps a small cake . . .'

'Right! Two teas, one cake and one sikisti!' he called out.

'What's a sikisti?' she asked.

'It's a hot egg sandwich. It's called sikisti because it costs sixty cents!'

She laughed.

'It's true, believe me!'

Akoto was a professor of sociology, from Ghana.

'What are you studying?' he asked her, after their tea.

'Literature.'

'Do you read any African writers?'

'Yes. Soyinka . . . Achebe . . .'

'*Things fall apart . . .*' he said.

'*The centre cannot hold.*' She finished the words for him.

He laughed. 'What about Ngugi? Palangyo? Omari?'

She shook her head. She hadn't heard of them.

'New, local writers. You should read Nuru Omari. *Wait for Me*, that's her first book. I could lend it to you if you want.'

'It's okay. I'll borrow it from the library.'

He looked very surprised. 'But it'll take a long time for the library to get it.'

'I'll wait . . . I don't have much time right now.'

'All right.' He was annoyed. At last, when he saw that she was a little restless, he said, 'Well, now that I've apologized, I hope . . . Well, perhaps we can go.'

I am studying literature and I have no time to read the most recent books, she thought. She felt ashamed.

When she saw him again several days later, he did not appear to notice her.

He knows I'm not interested, she thought. *So why did I go to the tea shop with him? . . . Because he's so different, so confident, so intelligent . . . He's a real gentleman! Ah, that's it! He said we Asians are westernized, but what about him? He's a perfect English gentleman himself! I'll tell him that!*

'Dear Professor Akoto,' she wrote, 'I wanted to tell you something. You called us Asians westernized. Well, have you looked at yourself recently? Your language, your clothes – a suit even in hot weather – you are just like an English gentleman yourself! Yours sincerely, Yasmin Rajan. P.S. Could I borrow Omari's *Wait for Me* from you after all? Thanks.' She put the note under his office door.

The next day he came to find her at lunchtime again.

'You're quite right,' he said. 'Although I'm not sure I completely agree . . . But let's not argue. Let me show you my library. You can borrow any book you like.'

He took her to his house, and when he opened the door of his sitting room, her eyes opened wide in surprise. Three of the walls were covered with books. She had never before seen so many books which belonged to one person.

'You've read all these books?' she asked.

'Well . . . I wouldn't . . .'

'Lucky you. You must know so much!'

'Oh, not really.'

'Do you also write?'

'Yes. But none of my writing is published yet.'

He had ideas about African literature. 'Today's writers are going back to their beginnings, digging deep. And that's what I'm trying to do – dig. So you can understand why I worry about what's real and what isn't.'

They went to The Matumbi that evening. She had her first sikisti, and talked about her family.

'My father had a pawnshop, but pawnshops are no longer allowed, so now he has a shop which makes men's clothes. Tell me, do you think pawnshops are a bad thing?'

'Well, I think they're bad for poor people. They have to pay an awful lot to get their things back.'

'But where *can* poor people borrow money from? Not the banks! And you should see the kind of things they bring to the pawnshop. Old watches, broken bicycles, sometimes clothes. We have three old gramophones that we can't sell.'

'Is that right? Can I look at them? Perhaps I'll buy one. I like unfashionable old things.'

So one afternoon Yasmin took him to her father's shop to show him the old gramophones. He entered the shop alone, while Yasmin went round to the back of the building, where the family lived. Her father came to meet Akoto.

'Come in, Bwana. What can I get for you?'

'I came with Yasmin,' Akoto explained in his bad Swahili. 'For a gramophone . . .'

'Ah, yes! The professor! Sit, Bwana, sit.'

While Yasmin's father showed Akoto the gramophones, Yasmin was inside the house, talking to her mother.

'How can you bring him here like this?' said her mother angrily. 'What will the neighbours think? I'm so ashamed!'

'But Mummy, he is a professor!'

'I don't care if he's a professor's father!'

By the time Akoto had left the shop, with his gramophone, Yasmin's mother was wild with anger. 'You do *not* have friendships with men – not with men who we don't know.'

'The world is not ready for it,' said Yasmin's father quietly.

'You stay out of it!' his wife screamed. 'This is between Yasmin and me!'

Yasmin knew her father would discuss things sensibly, but her mother never stopped warning her, and punishing her, and expecting the worst, just because she was a girl. Yasmin's three brothers did not have this problem.

'What do you know of him? With an Asian man, even if he's very bad, you know what to expect. But with *him*?' Her mother went on shouting and screaming like this for hours.

By the end of the day Yasmin felt half dead with tiredness.

It was more than a week before she and Akoto met again.

'Where do you eat lunch these days?' he said, smiling.

'You're the perfect salesman. You sell me an old gramophone and disappear. Are you afraid I'll return it?'

She said something polite, and walked quickly away. Later she returned the books that she had borrowed from him, and refused an invitation to The Matumbi. She did not go to the end-of-year dance, but her friends told her what happened there. Professor Akoto sat alone at a table for a while, and drank quite a lot. He got into a fight with Mr Sharp of the Boys' School. Then he left.

India was not just the past, or the close circle of family, neighbours, and friends. India was a place, a culture, one of the great nations of the world. And during the holidays Yasmin discovered India. She read endlessly, and asked her father about it. Here in Africa she was an Asian, an Indian. But up to now she had known almost nothing about India. At first, her search for her own past seemed to put a distance between her and Akoto, the African. But this was what he had talked about – digging deep, finding what was real. So in a strange way her search also brought her closer to him.

The world seemed a smaller place when she went back to university. Smaller but exciting; full of people doing their best, fighting, loving, staying alive. And she was one of those people. People who were locked into their own histories and customs were like prisoners, she thought. But sometimes the old patterns were broken, and things changed – lives changed, the world changed. She was part of that change, she decided.

A month later Yasmin's father was lifting boxes in his shop when he felt a pain in his heart. The doctor was called, but arrived late, and by then Yasmin's father was dead.

Daniel Akoto came to the funeral. He sat on the ground among the men, sweating and uncomfortable, trying to sit with his legs crossed. A black face in a sea of patient brown Asian faces.

Someone saw how uncomfortable he was and put out a chair for him by the wall. From there Akoto could see clearly across the room.

Mrs Rajan sat beside the dead man, crying. When she looked up, she saw Akoto through her tears, and lost control.

'You!' she screamed. 'What are you doing here? What kind of man are you, who comes to take away my daughter, even in my sadness? Who asked you to come? Go away!'

People turned to stare. Akoto gave an apologetic smile.

'Go!' said the woman wildly, pointing a finger at the door.

No one else said a word. Akoto stood up, bent his head respectfully towards the dead man and left the room.

A week later Yasmin knocked at his door late in the evening and found him in.

'Come in,' he said, putting away his pipe.

'I've come to apologize for what happened at the funeral.'

'It's all right. People aren't at their best at a funeral . . .

but perhaps they're more honest.' He watched her face carefully.

'You must think we're awful. You're a professor – you know so much – you're a great man . . .'

'No, I don't think you're awful. And don't call me a great man!'

She began to laugh, a little wildly. They both laughed.

'And you, I respect you.' He spoke calmly. 'You are brave. You left that crowd of girls that day at the dance, and since then you've done it again and again. It's brave, what you've done. Trying to break away from family, friends, the old customs, the old ways . . . trying to find your own path in life . . . Even coming here like this. I realize that and I like you.'

'Well, I like you too!' she said, too quickly. There was a silence between them. 'You know, it's not going to be easy . . . with my father dead, this will be the most terrible news for my mother . . . it will kill her, it will . . .' Tears were running down her face.

'Now, now.' He went up to her, put her wet face on his shirt. 'We'll have to do the best we can, won't we?'

WORD FOCUS

Match each word with an appropriate meaning. After the dance, perhaps
Yasmin spoke with her friends. Use five of the sixteen words to complete
the passage below. (Use one word in each gap.)

alcohol	ashamed, worried about what other people think	the ideas and beliefs of a particular society or country
apologize		
attack *(v & n)*	the study of human society and social behaviour	an old-fashioned machine for playing musical records
Bwana		
culture	a man of good family who always behaves well	an important university teacher
custom		to admire or have a high opinion of someone
embarrassed	the usual, accepted way of doing something in a society	writing, such as novels, plays and poetry
gentleman		
gramophone		drinks such as beer, wine, and whisky contain this
literature	a Swahili word used when speaking to an important man	to say that you are sorry for something that you have done
pawnshop		
professor	to lose water from your skin when you are hot or afraid	following ideas and ways of life that are typical of Western Europe and North America
respect		
sociology	to start fighting or hurting someone	a shop that lends money in exchange for something left with them (if you want it back, you must repay the money)
sweat *(v)*		
westernized		

'I was so _____ when I saw all of you looking at us and laughing! I
know I ought to _____ him because he's a _____ at the university. But
while we were dancing, he told me that the Asians here are too _____. I
didn't know what to say! I felt under _____, with everyone watching me.
I know it was rude, but I just had to walk away from him.'

STORY FOCUS

Here are four short passages from the story. Read them and answer the questions.

> '. . . you're too westernized, you Asians. You like Western ways, European ways, even more than we Africans do.'

1 Who is speaking, and to whom?
2 What do you think the speaker means by 'too westernized'?

> 'How can you bring him here like this? What will the neighbours think? I'm so ashamed!'

3 Who says these words in the story, and to whom?
4 Why do you think the speaker is 'ashamed'?

> 'The world is not ready for it.'

5 Who is speaking, and to whom?
6 What do you think the speaker means by 'the world is not ready for it' – not ready for what?

> 'It's brave, what you've done. Trying to break away from family, friends, the old customs, the old ways . . . trying to find your own path in life.'

7 Who says these words in the story, and to whom?
8 Do you agree with the speaker that the listener has been 'brave'? Explain your answer.

The Silk

It came from China, a piece of blue silk that lit up the room with its colours – the peacocks with their shining silvery tails, the blue lakes and the white waterfalls, the cloudy mountains and the dark blue trees. It was too lovely to wear, too beautiful to cut with scissors.

All through the long years of a marriage the silk had stayed safely in its box – waiting, but not forgotten. And now, the time had come . . .

JOY COWLEY

The Silk

Retold by Christine Lindop

When Mr Blackie became ill again that autumn, both he and Mrs Blackie knew that it was for the last time. For many weeks neither spoke of it; but the understanding was in their eyes as they watched each other through the days and nights. It was a look seen in the faces of the old and the very young, neither sad, nor hopeless, just a quiet understanding; they accepted what was coming.

It showed in other ways too. There were no more cross words from Mrs Blackie about her lazy old husband. Instead she took care of him day and night. She managed their money carefully to buy him his favourite foods; she let the district nurse visit him, but no more than twice a week.

Mr Blackie went to his bed and stayed there quietly. He had never talked much about the past, but now he spoke a lot about their earlier days. Sometimes, to Mrs Blackie's surprise, he remembered things that she had forgotten. He talked very little about the present, and never in those weeks about the future.

Then, on the first icy morning of the winter, while Mrs Blackie was filling his hot water bottle, he sat up in bed to see out the window. He could see a row of houses outside, with ice on the grass in front of them, like a white carpet.

'The ground will be hard,' he said at last. 'Hard as a rock.'

Mrs Blackie looked up quickly. 'Not yet,' she said.

'Soon, I think.' He smiled, but she knew he was saying sorry to her. She put the hot water bottle into its cover.

'Lie down or you'll catch cold,' she said.

He lay back against the pillow, but as she moved about him, putting the hot water bottle at his feet, he stared at the shapes of ice on the window.

'Amy, you'll get a double plot, won't you?' he said. 'I won't rest easy if I think that one day you're going to sleep by someone else.'

'What a thing to say!' The corners of her mouth moved suddenly. 'You know very well I won't do that.'

'It was your idea to buy single beds,' he said crossly.

'Oh, Herb—' She looked at the window, away again. 'We'll have a double plot.' For a second or two she waited by his bed, then she sat down beside his feet, with one hand resting on top of the other. This was the way that she always sat when she had something important to say.

'You know, I've been thinking on and off about the silk.'

'The silk?' He turned his head towards her.

'I want to use it for your laying-out pyjamas.'

'No, Amy,' he said. 'Not the silk. That was your wedding present, the only thing that I brought back with me.'

'What am I going to do with it now?' she said. When

he didn't answer, she got up, opened the cupboard door and took down the wooden box. 'All these years we've kept it. We should use it some time.'

'Not on me,' he said.

'I've been thinking about your pyjamas.' She fitted a key into the lock on the box. 'It'll be just right.'

'It'll be a right mistake, I think,' he said. But he could not keep the excitement out of his voice. He watched her hands as she opened the box, and pulled back the sheets of thin white paper. Below them lay the blue of the silk. They were both silent as she took it out and put it on the bed.

'Makes the whole room look different, doesn't it?' he said. 'I nearly forgot it looked like this.' His hands moved with difficulty across the bed cover. Gently she picked up the blue silk and let it fall in a river over his fingers.

'Aah,' he sighed, bringing it close to his eyes. 'All the way from China.' He smiled. 'I kept it on me all the time. You know that, Amy? There were people on that ship who wanted to steal that silk. But I kept it pinned round my middle.'

'You told me,' she said.

He held the silk against his face. 'It's the birds that you notice,' he said.

'At first,' said Mrs Blackie. She ran her finger over one of the peacocks that marched across the land of silk. They were beautiful birds, shining blue, with silver threads in their tails. 'I used to like them best, but after a while you see much more, just as fine, only smaller.' She pushed her glasses higher up her nose and looked closely at the silk, her eyes following her finger. She saw islands with waterfalls between little houses and dark blue trees; flat lakes with small fishing boats; mountains with their tops in silvery clouds; and back again to a peacock with one foot in the air above a rock.

'They just don't make anything as beautiful as this in this country,' she said.

Mr Blackie held up the box, enjoying the smell of the wood. 'Don't cut it, Amy. It's too good for someone like me.' But his eyes were asking her to disagree with him.

'I'll get the pattern tomorrow,' she said.

The next day, while the district nurse was giving him his injection, she went down to the store and chose a pattern from the pattern books. Mr Blackie, who had worn boring pyjamas all his life, looked at the picture of the young man on the front of the packet and crossed his arms.

'What's this – a Chinese suit? That's young men's clothes, not suitable for me,' he said.

'Rubbish,' said Mrs Blackie.

'Modern rubbish,' he said, 'that's what it is. You're never putting those on me.'

'It's not your job to decide,' said Mrs Blackie.

'Not my job? I'll get up and fight – you wait and see.'

'All right, Herb, if you really don't like it—'

But now he had won, he was happy. 'Oh, go on, Amy. It's not such a bad idea. In fact, I think they're fine. It's that nurse, you see. The injection hurt.' He looked at the pattern. 'When do you start?'

'Well—'

'This afternoon?'

'I could pin the pattern out after lunch, I suppose.'

'Do it in here,' he said. 'Bring in your machine and pins and things so I can watch.'

She turned her head and looked at him. 'I'm not using the machine,' she said. 'I'm doing it all by hand – every thread of it. My eyes aren't as good as they were, but nobody in this world can say that I'm not still good with my needle.'

His eyes closed as he thought. 'How long?'

'Eh?'

'Until it's finished.'

She turned the pattern over in her hands. 'Oh – about three or four weeks. That is – if I work hard.'

'No,' he said. 'Too long.'

'Oh, Herb, you want me to do a good job, don't you?' she said.

'Amy—' He shook his head on the pillow.

'I can use the machine for some of it,' she said, in a quieter voice.

'How long?'

'A week,' she whispered.

Although the doctor had told him to lie flat in bed, he made her give him another pillow that afternoon. She took the pillow from her own bed, shook it, and put it behind his neck. Then she measured his body, legs, and arms.

'I'll have to make them a bit smaller,' she said, writing

down big black numbers. Mr Blackie was waiting, his eyes wide. He looked brighter, she thought, than he had for weeks.

As she arranged the silk on her bed and started pinning the first of the pattern pieces, he described the journey home by boat, the stop at Hong Kong, and the man who had sold him the silk.

'Most of it was rubbish,' he said. 'This was the only good thing that he had, and I still paid too much for it. You got to argue with these people, they told me. But there were others who wanted that silk, and I had to buy it – or lose it.' He looked at her hands. 'What are you doing now? You just put that bit down.'

'It wasn't right,' she said, through lips closed on pins. 'It needs to be in just the right place. I have to join a tree to a tree, not to the middle of a waterfall.'

She lifted the pattern pieces many times before everything was right. Then it was evening, and Mr Blackie could talk no more. He lay back on his pillows, his eyes red from tiredness.

'Go to sleep,' she said. 'Enough's enough for one day.'

'I want you to cut it out first,' he said.

'Let's leave it until the morning,' she said, and they both knew that she did not want to put the scissors to the silk.

'Tonight,' he said.

'I'll make the tea first.'

'After,' he said.

She picked up the scissors and held them for a moment.

Then together they felt the pain as the scissors closed cleanly in that first cut. The silk would never again be the same. They were changing it, arranging the pattern of some fifty years to make something new and different. When she had cut out the first piece, she held it up, still pinned to the paper, and said, 'The back of the top.' Then she put it down and went on as quickly as she could, because she knew that he would not rest until she had finished.

One by one the pieces left the body of silk. Each time the scissors moved, mountains fell in half, peacocks were cut from head to tail. In the end, there was nothing on the bed but a few shining threads. Mrs Blackie picked them up and put them back in the wooden box. Then she took her pillow from Mr Blackie's bed and made him comfortable before she went into the kitchen to make the tea.

He was very tired the next morning, but refused to sleep while she was working with the silk. From time to time she thought of a reason to leave the room. He slept then, but never for long. After no more than half an hour, he would call. She would find him awake, waiting for her to start again.

In that day and the next, she did all the machine work. It was a long, boring job, because first she sewed all the pieces in place by hand. Mr Blackie silently watched every move she made. Sometimes she saw him studying the silk, and on his face was a look that she remembered. It was the way that he had looked at her when they were young lovers. That hurt a little. He didn't care about the silk more than he cared about her, she knew that, but he saw something in it that she didn't. She never asked him what it was. Someone of her age did not question these things or ask for explanations. She just went on with the work, thinking only of the sewing and the silk.

On the Friday afternoon, four days after she'd started the pyjamas, she finished the buttonholes and sewed on the buttons. She had had to work more quickly at the end. In the four days Mr Blackie had become weaker. She knew that when the pyjamas were finished and put back in the box, he would be more interested in food and rest.

She cut the last thread and put away the needle.

'That's it, Herb,' she said, showing him her work.

He tried to lift his head. 'Bring them over here,' he said.

'Well – what do you think?' As she brought the pyjamas closer, he saw them clearly and he smiled.

'Try them on?' he said.

She shook her head. 'I measured you carefully,' she said. 'They'll fit.'

'We should make sure,' he said.

Why didn't she want him to try them on? She couldn't find a reason. 'All right,' she said, turning on the heater. 'Just to make sure the buttons are right.'

She took off his thick pyjamas and put on the silk. She stepped back to look at him.

'Well, I have to say that's a fine job. I could move the top button a little bit, but really they fit beautifully.'

He smiled at her. 'Light, aren't they?' He looked all

down his body and moved his toes. 'All the way from China. I kept it with me day and night. Know that, Amy?'

'Do you like them?'

He tried not to look too pleased. 'All right. A little bit small.'

'They are not, and you know it,' Mrs Blackie said crossly. 'It wouldn't hurt to say thank you. Here, put your hands down and I'll change you before you get cold.'

He crossed his arms. 'You did a really good job, Amy. Think I'll keep them on for a bit.'

'No.' She picked up his thick pyjamas.

'Why not?'

'Because you can't,' she said. 'It – it's not the right thing to do. And the nurse will be here soon.'

'Oh, you and your ideas.' He was too weak to stop her, but as she changed him, he still could not take his eyes away from the silk. 'Wonder who made it?'

She didn't answer, but a picture came to her of a Chinese woman sitting at a machine making silk. She was dressed in beautiful Eastern clothes, and although she had Eastern eyes, she looked like Mrs Blackie.

'Do you think there are places like that?' Mr Blackie asked.

She picked the pyjamas up quickly and put them in the box. 'You're the one who's been to the East,' she said. 'Now get some rest or you'll be tired when the nurse arrives.'

The district nurse did not come that afternoon. Nor in the evening. It was half-past three the next morning when

Mrs Blackie heard the nurse's footsteps, and the doctor's, outside the house.

She was in the kitchen, waiting. She sat with straight back and dry eyes, with one hand resting on top of the other.

'Mrs Blackie, I'm sorry—'

She didn't answer and turned to the doctor. 'He didn't say goodbye,' she said, her voice angry. 'Just before I phoned. His hand was over the side of the bed. I touched it. It was cold.'

The doctor nodded.

'No sound of any kind,' she said. 'He was fine last night.'

Again the doctor nodded. He put his hand on her shoulder for a moment, then went into the bedroom. A minute later he returned, closing his bag, speaking kindly.

Mrs Blackie sat still, hearing words. Peacefully. Brave. The words dropped onto her. They didn't seem to mean anything.

'He didn't say goodbye.' She shook her head. 'Not a word.'

'But look, Mrs Blackie,' the nurse said gently. 'It was going to happen. You know that. He was—'

'I know, I know.' She turned away crossly. Why didn't they understand? 'I just wanted him to say goodbye. That's all.'

The doctor offered her something to help her sleep but she pushed it away. And she refused the cup of tea that the district nurse put in front of her. When they picked up their bags and went towards the bedroom, she followed them.

'In a few minutes,' the doctor said. 'If you'll leave us—'

'I'm getting his pyjamas,' she said. 'I need to change a button. I can do it now.'

When she entered the room, she looked at Mr Blackie's bed and saw that the doctor had pulled up the sheet. Quickly, she lifted the wooden box, took a needle, thread, scissors, her glasses, and went back to the kitchen. Through the door she heard the nurse's voice, 'Poor old thing,' and she knew that they were not talking about her.

She sat down at the table to thread the needle. Her eyes were clear, but for a long time her hands refused to obey her.

At last, her needle and thread ready, she opened the wooden box. The beauty of the silk always surprised her. As she arranged the pyjamas on the table, she was filled with a strong, warm feeling, the first good feeling that she had had that morning. The silk was real. The light above the table filled everything with life. Trees moved above the water, peacocks danced with white fire in their tails. And the little bridges . . .

Mrs Blackie took off her glasses, cleaned them, put them on again. She sat down and touched one bridge with her finger, then another. And another. She turned over the pyjama coat and looked carefully at the back. It was there, on every bridge; something she hadn't noticed before. She got up and fetched her magnifying glass.

As the bridge in the pattern on the silk grew, the little

group of threads, which had been no bigger than a grain of rice, became a man.

Mrs Blackie forgot about the button, and the quiet voices in the bedroom. She brought the magnifying glass nearer her eyes.

It was a man, and he was standing with one arm held out on the highest part of the bridge between two islands. Mrs Blackie studied him for a long time, then she sat up and smiled. Yes, he was waving. Or perhaps, she thought, he was calling her to join him.

WORD FOCUS

Use the clues below and complete this crossword with words from the story.

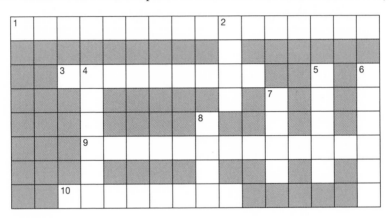

ACROSS

1 Mrs Blackie used the silk to make Mr Blackie's _____ _____ _____, the clothes he would wear when he was buried. *(3 words)*

3 The nurse gave Mr Blackie an _____, putting medicine into his body with a needle.

9 The _____ _____ visits sick people in their homes, and she visited Mr Blackie at home twice a week. *(2 words)*

10 The large birds with blue and silver tails on the silk were _____.

DOWN

2 Mr Blackie asked to be buried in a double _____, because he wanted Mrs Blackie to be buried beside him when she died.

4 and 6 Mrs Blackie wanted to make the pyjamas by hand using only a _____ and _____, but Mr Blackie said it would take too long.

5 Mrs Blackie went to the _____ to buy a pattern for the pyjamas.

7 Mrs Blackie used _____, short pieces of metal with sharp points, to put the pattern onto the silk.

8 _____ is a kind of fine smooth cloth made from silkworm threads.

Story Focus

Read the three endings for each of these sentences. All the endings are possible, but which one best goes with your understanding of the story? Choose one of them, and explain why you chose it.

1 Mrs Blackie allowed the district nurse to visit Mr Blackie no more than twice a week because . . .

a) they didn't have enough money to pay for more visits.

b) she didn't like the nurse.

c) she knew that her husband was dying and wanted him to have peace.

2 Mrs Blackie wanted to use the silk to make the laying-out pyjamas for her husband because . . .

a) she didn't want to spend money buying other materials.

b) Mr Blackie brought it from China as a wedding present for her.

c) she thought it was very beautiful.

3 Mrs Blackie wanted to make the pyjamas by hand, using only a needle and thread, but Mr Blackie didn't like this idea because . . .

a) he knew he would not live long enough to see them.

b) he didn't want his wife to work too hard.

c) he thought she could do a better job with the sewing machine.

4 Mr Blackie didn't say goodbye to his wife because . . .

a) he was too weak and could not speak.

b) he knew that Mrs Blackie would see the little man on the bridge and would know that he loved her and was waiting for her.

c) he was angry that the pyjamas were too small.

About the
Authors

~

JANET TAY HUI CHING

Janet Tay Hui Ching (1976–) was born in Malaysia, and was educated in Sarawak and at university in England. She lives in Kuala Lumpur, Malaysia. She began her working life as an advocate and solicitor, but after five years she left the legal profession and became a book editor at a local publishing house.

The idea for her story *Callus* came to her during a party for her grandmother's birthday. She was listening to her relatives talking about the 1940s when it was legal to have two wives, and she began to wonder how a first wife would feel if her husband married a second wife.

JACKEE BUDESTA BATANDA

Jackee Budesta Batanda was born in Uganda, and lives in Kampala. She read a lot as a child, and at the age of fourteen, she decided to be a writer because she wanted 'to create stories that captivate and enchant readers around the world'. She has been Writer-in-Residence at Lancaster University, England, and Peace Writer at the University of San Diego, California.

Her short stories have appeared in many publications and in radio broadcasts, and won several prizes. She has written a children's book, *The Blue Marble*, a collection of short stories, *Everyday People*, and is currently at work on a novel.

O. HENRY

O. Henry (1862–1910), whose real name was William Sydney Porter, was born in North Carolina in the USA. When he was twenty, he went to Texas and worked in many different offices and then in a bank. In 1887 he married a young woman called Athol Estes, and he and Athol were very happy together. His most famous short story is *The Gift of the Magi*, and many people think that Della in that story is based on his wife Athol.

In 1896 Porter ran away to Honduras because people said he stole money from the bank when he was working there in 1894. A year later he came back to Texas to see his wife Athol, who was dying, and in 1898 he was sent to prison. During his time there he published many short stories, and when he left prison in 1901, he was already a famous writer.

Porter's stories are both sad and funny, and show a great understanding of the everyday lives of ordinary people. He wrote about six hundred stories and made a lot of money, but he was a very unhappy man. When he died, he had only twenty-three cents in his pocket, and his last words were:

'Turn up the lights; I don't want to go home in the dark.'

EDGAR ALLAN POE

Edgar Allan Poe (1809–1849) was born in Boston, USA. His parents died when he was young, and he went to live with the Allan family in Richmond. He spent a year at university and then two years in the army. In 1831, he moved to Baltimore to live with his aunt and his cousin Virginia. For the next few years, life was difficult. He sold some stories to magazines, but they brought him little money. But he did find happiness with Virginia, whom he married in 1836.

From 1838 to 1844, Poe lived in Philadelphia, where he wrote some of his most famous horror stories. Then he moved to New York, where his poem, *The Raven*, soon made him famous. But Virginia died in 1847, and Poe began drinking heavily. He tried to kill himself in 1848 and died the following year.

Poe wrote many different kinds of stories, and his horror stories are only a small portion of his work. But to most people the name Edgar Allan Poe means stories of death and madness, horror and ghosts.

SAKI

Hector Hugh Monro (1870–1916), the British writer known as Saki, was born in Burma (now known as Myanmar). After his mother died, he and his sister and brother went to live with their two aunts in England. Aunt Tom and Aunt Augusta hated each other and were not interested in children. So, like the children in *The Story-Teller*, Saki learned to dislike aunts. He often dreamed and wrote of a world where animals were stronger than people and could punish them for being cruel and stupid.

In 1893 Saki joined the army in Burma, but became ill and returned to London three years later. He then worked as a journalist for *The Morning Post*, travelling in France, Poland, and Russia. When the First World War began, he joined the army, and was killed in France in 1916.

He is best known today for his short stories, which are both cruel and funny at the same time. He published five collections of short stories and two novels.

M. G. VASSANJI

M. G. Vassanji (1950–) was born in Nairobi, Kenya, to an Indian family, and brought up in Tanzania. He now lives in Toronto, Canada, and visits Africa and India often. He studied at the Massachusetts Institute of Technology and the University of Pennsylvania in the USA, then moved to Canada in 1978. After the success of his first novel, *The Gunny Sack* (1989), he became a full-time writer, and so far has written six novels, and two collections of short stories, *Uhuru Street* (1990) and *When She Was Queen* (2005). His work has won several prizes, and deals with Indians living in East Africa. He says: 'Once I went to the US, suddenly the Indian connection became very important; the sense of origins, trying to understand the roots of India that we had inside us.'

JOY COWLEY

Joy Cowley (1936–) found reading difficult as a child, but when she discovered the adventures that could be found in books, she became a reading addict. She began writing stories in the evenings while working as a farmer's wife and bringing up four children. Now she sees herself as a wife, mother, grandmother, and great-grandmother. This is who she is; writing is what she does, and she was been writing for nearly fifty years.

She has written many short stories and novels for adults, more than 600 books for children, and has won a great number of awards. One of her children's books, *Mrs Wishy-Washy's Farm*, has sold more than forty million copies worldwide. She still writes for both children and adults, and spends a lot of time at conferences, workshops, and helping other writers. However, she spends most of her time 'answering letters from young friends all over the world, a task that I consider to be more play than work.'

READING CIRCLE ROLES

When you work on your role sheet, remember these words:
~ READ ~ THINK ~ CONNECT ~ ASK ~~ AND CONNECT

READ ~
- Read the story once without stopping.
- Read it again while you work on your role sheet.

THINK ~
- Look for passages in the story that are interesting or unusual. Think about them. Prepare some questions to ask about them.
- Think about the meanings of words. If you use a dictionary, try to use an English-to-English learner's dictionary.

CONNECT ~
- Connect with the characters' thoughts and feelings. Perhaps it is a horror story and we cannot 'connect' with an experience like this, but we can see how the characters are thinking or feeling.

ASK ~
- Ask questions with many possible answers; questions that begin with *How? Why? What? Who?* Do not ask *yes/no* questions.
- When you ask questions, use English words that everyone in your circle can understand, so that everyone can talk about the story.

AND CONNECT ~
- Connect with your circle. Share your ideas, listen to other people's ideas. If you don't understand something, ask people to repeat or explain. And have fun!

The role sheets are on the next six pages (and on page 97 there are role badges you can make). Bigger role sheets, with space for writing, are in the Teacher's Handbook. Or you can read about your role in these pages, and write your notes and questions in your own notebook.

Discussion Leader

STORY: _____

NAME: _____

The Discussion Leader's job is to . . .

- read the story twice, and prepare at least five general questions about it.
- ask one or two questions to start the Reading Circle discussion.
- make sure that everyone has a chance to speak and joins in the discussion.
- call on each member to present their prepared role information.
- guide the discussion and keep it going.

Usually the best discussion questions come from your own thoughts, feelings, and questions as you read. (What surprised you, made you smile, made you feel sad?) Write down your questions as soon as you have finished reading. It is best to use your own questions, but you can also use some of the ideas at the bottom of this page.

MY QUESTIONS:

1 _____

_____

_____

_____

_____

_____

_____

_____

Other general ideas:

- Questions about the characters (*like / not like them, true to life / not true to life ...?*)
- Questions about the theme (*friendship, romance, parents /children, ghosts ...?*)
- Questions about the ending (*surprising, expected, liked it / did not like it ...?*)
- Questions about what will happen next. (These can also be used for a longer story.)

Summarizer

STORY: _____

NAME: _____

The Summarizer's job is to . . .

- read the story and make notes about the characters, events, and ideas.
- find the key points that everyone must know to understand and remember the story.
- retell the story in a short summary (one or two minutes) in your own words.
- talk about your summary to the group, using your writing to help you.

Your reading circle will find your summary very useful, because it will help to remind them of the plot and the characters in the story. You may need to read the story more than once to make a good summary, and you may need to repeat it to the group a second time.

MY KEY POINTS:

Main events:

Characters:

MY SUMMARY:

Connector

STORY: _____

NAME: _____

The Connector's job is to . . .

- read the story twice, and look for connections between the story and the world outside.
- make notes about at least two possible connections to your own experiences, or to the experiences of friends and family, or to real-life events.
- tell the group about the connections and ask for their comments or questions.
- ask the group if they can think of any connections themselves.

These questions will help you think about connections while you are reading.

Events: Has anything similar ever happened to you, or to someone you know? Does anything in the story remind you of events in the real world? For example, events you have read about in newspapers, or heard about on television news programmes.

Characters: Do any of them remind you of people you know? How? Why? Have you ever had the same thoughts or feelings as these characters have? Do you know anybody who thinks, feels, behaves like that?

MY CONNECTIONS:

1 _____

_____

_____

_____

_____

_____

_____

_____

_____

_____

Word Master

STORY: _____

NAME: _____

The Word Master's job is to . . .

- read the story, and look for words or short phrases that are new or difficult to understand, or that are important in the story.
- choose five words (only five) that you think are important for this story.
- explain the meanings of these five words in simple English to the group.
- tell the group why these words are important for understanding this story.

Your five words do not have to be new or unknown words. Look for words in the story that really stand out in some way. These may be words that are:

- repeated often
- used in an unusual way
- important to the meaning of the story

MY WORDS	MEANING OF THE WORD	REASON FOR CHOOSING THE WORD
PAGE _____ **LINE** _____		
PAGE _____ **LINE** _____		
PAGE _____ **LINE** _____		
PAGE _____ **LINE** _____		
PAGE _____ **LINE** _____		

Passage Person

STORY: _____

NAME: _____

The Passage Person's job is to . . .

- read the story, and find important, interesting, or difficult passages.
- make notes about at least three passages that are important for the plot, or that explain the characters, or that have very interesting or powerful language.
- read each passage to the group, or ask another group member to read it.
- ask the group one or two questions about each passage.

A passage is usually one paragraph, but sometimes it can be just one or two sentences, or perhaps a piece of dialogue. You might choose a passage to discuss because it is:

• important • informative • surprising • funny • confusing • well-written

MY PASSAGES:

PAGE _____ LINES _____

REASONS FOR CHOOSING THE PASSAGE	QUESTIONS ABOUT THE PASSAGE

PAGE _____ LINES _____

REASONS FOR CHOOSING THE PASSAGE	QUESTIONS ABOUT THE PASSAGE

PAGE _____ LINES _____

REASONS FOR CHOOSING THE PASSAGE	QUESTIONS ABOUT THE PASSAGE

Culture Collector

STORY: _____

NAME: _____

The Culture Collector's job is to . . .

- read the story, and look for both differences and similarities between your own culture and the culture found in the story.
- make notes about two or three passages that show these cultural points.
- read each passage to the group, or ask another group member to read it.
- ask the group some questions about these, and any other cultural points in the story.

Here are some questions to help you think about cultural differences.

Theme: What is the theme of this story (for example, getting married, meeting a ghost, murder, unhappy children)? Is this an important theme in your own culture? Do people think about this theme in the same way, or differently?

People: Do characters in this story say or do things that people never say or do in your culture? Do they say or do some things that everybody in the world says or does?

MY CULTURAL COLLECTION (differences and similarities):

1 PAGE _____ LINES _____ : _____

_____

2 PAGE _____ LINES _____ : _____

_____

MY CULTURAL QUESTIONS:

— _____

— _____

— _____

— _____

PLOT PYRAMID ACTIVITY

A **plot** is a series of events which form a story. The Reading Circles **Plot Pyramid** is a way of looking at and talking about the plot of a story. The pyramid divides the story into five parts.

The Exposition gives the background needed to understand the story. It tells us who the characters are, where the story happens, and when it happens. Sometimes we also get an idea about problems to come.

The Complication is the single event which begins the conflict, or creates the problem. The event might be an action, a thought, or words spoken by one of the characters.

The Rising Action brings more events and difficulties. As the story moves through these events, it gets more exciting, and begins to take us toward the climax.

The Climax is the high point of the story, the turning point, the point of no return. It marks a change, for better or for worse, in the lives of one or more of the characters.

The Resolution usually offers an answer to the problem or the conflict, which may be sad or happy for the characters. Mysteries are explained, secrets told, and the reader can feel calm again.

HOW TO PLOT THE PYRAMID

1 Read your story again, and look for each part of the pyramid as you read. Make notes, or mark your book.

2 In your Reading Circle, find each part of the pyramid in the story, and then write down your ideas. Use the boxes in the diagram opposite as a guide (a bigger diagram, with space for writing in the boxes, is in the Teacher's Handbook).

3 Begin with the *Exposition*, and work through the *Complication*, the *Rising Action* (only two points), the *Climax*, and the *Resolution*.

4 Finally, your group draws the pyramid and writes the notes on the board, and then presents the pyramid to the class.

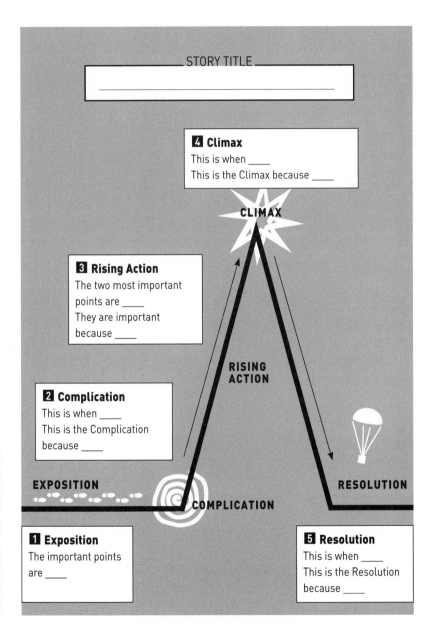

POSTER ACTIVITY

Each Reading Circle group makes a poster in English about a story in this book. Posters can have words, pictures, and drawings. Your group will need to find extra information about the story – perhaps from the Internet, or the school library, or your teacher.

Use the ideas on the opposite page to help you. When all the posters are finished, each Reading Circle will present their own poster to the other groups. At the end, keep all the posters, and make a 'poster library'.

_____ STORY TITLE _____

THE THEME

What is the theme of the story?

- Is it about love or murder or friendship? Is it about dreams or wishes or fears?

THE TIME, THE PLACE

What do you know about the time and the place of the story?

- the city / the country?
- a real world, or an unreal world?
- If the time and place are not given, does it matter?

THE WRITER

What interesting facts do you know about the author's life?

- Was he or she also a poet, an actor, a teacher? Or a spy, a sailor, a thief, a doctor, a madman?

THE BACKGROUND

What cultural information did you learn from the story?

- About family events (for example, a wedding)
- A national holiday
- Family life (for example, parents and children)

THE LANGUAGE

What did you like about the language in the story?

- Find a quotation you like – words that are funny or clever or sad, or words that paint a picture in your mind.

THE FILM

Direct your own film! Who will play the characters in the film?

- Choose the best actors to play the characters.
- Where will you film it?
- Will you change the story?
- What title will the film have?

BOOKWORMS CLUB
Stories for Reading Circles
The Metals Set

BOOKWORMS CLUB BRONZE   STAGES 1 AND 2

The Horse of Death by Sait Faik
The Little Hunters at the Lake by Yalvac Ural
Mr Harris and the Night Train by Jennifer Bassett
Sister Love by John Escott
Omega File 349: London, England by Jennifer Bassett
Tildy's Moment by O. Henry
Andrew, Jane, the Parson, and the Fox by Thomas Hardy

BOOKWORMS CLUB SILVER   STAGES 2 AND 3

The Christmas Presents by O. Henry
Netty Sargent and the House by Thomas Hardy
Too Old to Rock and Roll by Jan Mark
A Walk in Amnesia by O. Henry
The Five Orange Pips by Sir Arthur Conan Doyle
The Tell-Tale Heart by Edgar Allan Poe
Go, Lovely Rose by H. E. Bates

BOOKWORMS CLUB GOLD   STAGES 3 AND 4

The Black Cat by Edgar Allan Poe
Sredni Vashtar by Saki
The Railway Crossing by Freeman Wills Crofts
The Daffodil Sky by H. E. Bates
A Moment of Madness by Thomas Hardy
The Secret by Arthur C. Clarke
The Experiment by M. R. James

BOOKWORMS CLUB PLATINUM   STAGES 4 AND 5

No Morning After by Arthur C. Clarke
The Nine Billion Names of God by Arthur C. Clarke
Across the Australian Desert by Robyn Davidson
Casting the Runes by M. R. James
The Songs of Distant Earth by Arthur C. Clarke
Feuille d'Album by Katherine Mansfield
The Doll's House by Katherine Mansfield

BOOKWORMS CLUB
Stories for Reading Circles
The Gems Set

BOOKWORMS CLUB PEARL STAGES 2 AND 3
Callus by Janet Tay Hui Ching
Dora's Turn by Jackee Budesta Batanda
The Memento by O. Henry
The Cask of Amontillado by Edgar Allan Poe
The Story-Teller by Saki
Breaking Loose by M. G. Vassanji
The Silk by Joy Cowley

BOOKWORMS CLUB CORAL STAGES 3 AND 4
Gathering of the Whakapapa by Witi Ihimaera
The Waxwork by A. M. Burrage
The Glorious Pacific Way by Epeli Hau'ofa
A Kind of Longing by Philip Mincher
Missiya, the Wild One by Vijita Fernando
The Stepmother by Anne Ranasinghe
Because of the Rusilla by Mena Abdullah & Ray Mathew

BOOKWORMS CLUB RUBY STAGES 4 AND 5
Carapace by Romesh Gunesekera
A Devoted Son by Anita Desai
The Intelligence of Wild Things by Chitra Banerjee Divakaruni
Going Home by Archie Weller
My Oedipus Complex by Frank O'Connor
Irish Revel by Edna O'Brien
The Judge's House by Bram Stoker

BOOKWORMS CLUB DIAMOND STAGES 5 AND 6
Millie by Katherine Mansfield
Her First Ball by Katherine Mansfield
Men and Women by Claire Keegan
Mr Sing My Heart's Delight by Brian Friel
Death Wish by Lawrence Block
Cooking the Books by Christopher Fowler
The Stolen Body by H. G. Wells

ROLE BADGES

These role icons can be photocopied and then cut out to make badges or stickers for the members of the Reading Circle to wear.

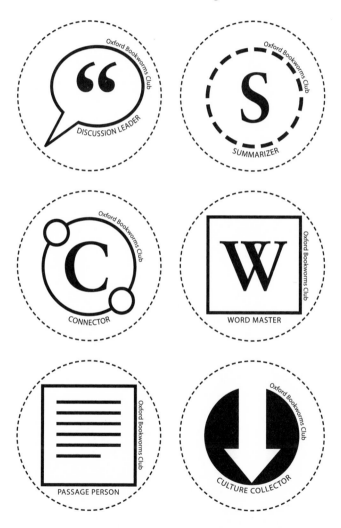